THE OFFICIAL CELTIC ANNUAL 2015

THE CELTIC FOOTBALL CLUB 1888

Written by Joe Sullivan & Mark Henderson
Designed by Chris Dalrymple

£7.99

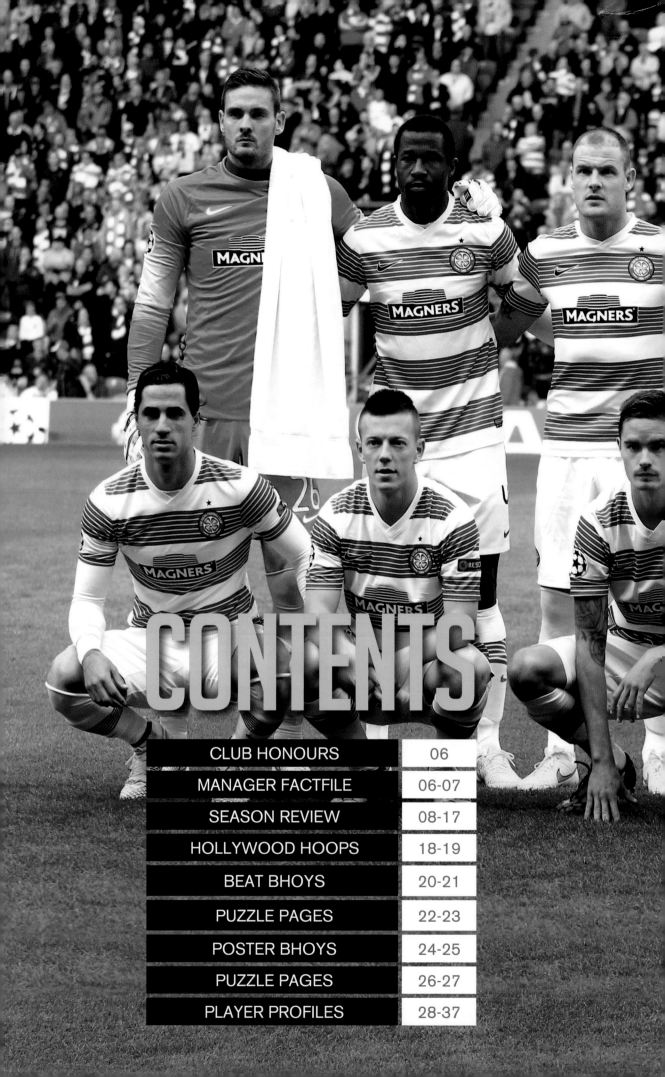

CONTENTS

CLUB HONOURS

MANAGER FACTFILE

NORWEGIAN Ronny Deila was the natural choice to follow Neil Lennon and become the 17th manager of Celtic given his spectacular success at former club Stromsgodset.

After taking the helm at the Drammen-based side in 2008, he quickly transformed the small club's fortunes, guiding them to national cup glory just two years later.

SCOTTISH LEAGUE WINNERS [45 TIMES]				
1892/93	1893/94	1895/96	1897/98	1904/05
1905/06	1906/07	1907/08	1908/09	1909/10
1913/14	1914/15	1915/16	1916/17	1918/19
1921/22	1925/26	1935/36	1937/38	1953/54
1965/66	1966/67	1967/68	1968/69	1969/70
1970/71	1971/72	1972/73	1973/74	1976/77
1978/79	1980/81	1981/82	1985/86	1987/88
1997/98	2000/01	2001/02	2003/04	2005/06
2006/07	2007/08	2011/12	2012/13	2013/14

SCOTTISH CUP WINNERS [36 TIMES]					
1892	1899	1900	1904	1907	1908
1911	1912	1914	1923	1925	1927
1931	1933	1937	1951	1954	1965
1967	1969	1971	1972	1974	1975
1977	1980	1985	1988	1989	1995
2001	2004	2005	2007	2011	2013

LEAGUE CUP WINNERS [14 TIMES]				
1956/57	1957/58	1965/66	1966/67	1967/68
1968/69	1969/70	1974/75	1982/83	1997/98
1999/00	2000/01	2005/06	2008/09	

EUROPEAN CUP WINNERS
1967

CORONATION CUP WINNERS
1953

And in 2013, remarkably, he inspired them to their first league championship in 42 years, beating off competition from the established clubs in Norway.

What's more, it was achieved by playing entertaining, attacking, high-intensity football, in a team comprised mostly of talented youngsters. These fantastic feats made him one of the most highly-rated young managers in European football.

A former Norway Under-21 internationalist, Ronny Deila spent his entire playing career in his homeland, making 240 appearances for Odd Grenland over 11 years – where he won the Norwegian Cup – before concluding his career with stints at Viking and Stromsgodset.

A qualified teacher, he is renowned for his progressive, forward-thinking approach and man-management skills.

He has also won acclaim for his ability to develop youngsters into top-class players, including current Celtic midfielder Stefan Johansen, who has flourished in Paradise since his arrival at the start of 2014.

These attributes have seen him compared to Borussia Dortmund coach Jurgen Klopp, someone the Norwegian has huge admiration for and who he has spent time with, studying his methods.

All this hadn't gone unnoticed in Paradise, and once Neil Lennon announced he was departing the club at the end of the 2013/14 season, the 38-year-old was immediately identified as the perfect candidate to take the club forward.

On June 6, 2014, Ronny Deila was confirmed as Celtic manager and immediately spoke of his determination to deliver attacking, exciting and attractive football to the Hoops faithful, and ultimately, win further silverware for the Scottish champions.

It's the start of a new journey in Paradise as the new Hoops boss aims to continue the club's dominance of the domestic game – and do it in the Celtic Way.

RONNY DEILA

D.O.B: 21/09/75

Born: Porsgrunn

Playing career record:
Odd Grenland (1993-2004)
Viking (2005)
Stromsgodset (2006-2008)

Playing honours:
Odd Grenland: Norwegian Cup Winners (2000)

As manager:
Norwegian Cup Winners (2010)
Norwegian Premier League Champions (2013)

THAT'S WHY WE'RE CHAMPIONS

AUGUST

CELTIC	2	1	ROSS COUNTY	STOKES 2
ABERDEEN	0	2	CELTIC	COMMONS, FORREST
CELTIC	2	2	INVERNESS CT	MULGREW, MATTHEWS
DUNDEE UTD	0	1	CELTIC	STOKES

CELTIC kicked off their UEFA Champions League campaign in July and before the end of August disposed of Cliftonville, IF Elfsborg and Shakhter Karagandy, although it took a last-minute clincher from James Forrest against the Kazakhstan side to seal group stage action.

Flag Day brought Ross County to Celtic Park and they almost proved to be party-poopers when they took the lead after only three minutes. Thankfully, just three minutes from the end, Anthony Stokes scored the winner in what proved to be the first of many victories for the Hoops.

Aberdeen also proved a tough nut to crack but goals late in each half gave the Hoops a 2-0 win, however there was a slight blip in the following game when the Celts had to come from 2-0 down to draw 2-2 with Inverness CT at home.

The month finished on a high, though, as just days after the last-gasp Karagandy

win, another goal three minutes from the end by Stokes gave Celtic a tight 1-0 victory over Dundee United at Tannadice.

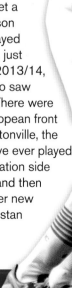

FAMOUS FIRSTS

IN 50 years of European football, Celtic never met a Swedish side until season 2012/13 when they played Helsingborgs, but then, just twelve months later in 2013/14, the luck of the draw also saw them play IF Elfsborg. There were further firsts on the European front when Celtic played Cliftonville, the first time the Hoops have ever played an Irish Football Association side in a competitive game and then in the next round another new destination was Kazakhstan where Celtic took on Shakhter Karagandy.

THE ROAD TO THREE-IN-A-ROW

SEPTEMBER

HEARTS	1	3	CELTIC	COMMONS, STOKES, PUKKI
CELTIC	2	1	ST JOHNSTONE	PUKKI, MULGREW
KILMARNOCK	2	5	CELTIC	SAMARAS 3, COMMONS, BALDE

PROGRESS to the Champions League group stages saw Celtic in the toughest of them all – the Group of Champions with fellow former winners Barcelona, AC Milan and Ajax, but cup competitions didn't favour the Hoops during the month of September.

Aside from losing 2-0 to AC Milan in Italy, hardly a surprise, there was a shock in store in the League Cup when Morton visited Celtic Park for a Tuesday night fixture where a penalty, during extra-time, gave the Greenock side a 1-0 win.

However, it was business as usual on the league front with new signing, Teemu Pukki, netting on his debut with the final goal in a 3-1 win over Hearts at Tynecastle. Then he did likewise in his second league outing by scoring the opener in a 2-1 home win over St Johnstone.

Rugby Park was next on the agenda and although Kris Commons and Amido Balde got the first and last goals against Kilmarnock, the star of the show was Georgios Samaras with the Greek striker firing in a hat-trick in the 5-2 win.

WHO'S WHO IN THE HOOPS

EACH of the sides Celtic met in domestic action this month at one time or another in their history wore the Hoops. Hearts wore red and blue Hoops on a white background in their early days and had maroon and white in the late 1920s. St Johnstone started off with thin black and white Hoops, similar to Queen's Park, and fluctuated with blue and white Hoops from 1905 until 1922. Morton have famously worn blue and white Hoops throughout their existence and Kilmarnock have done likewise for many seasons.

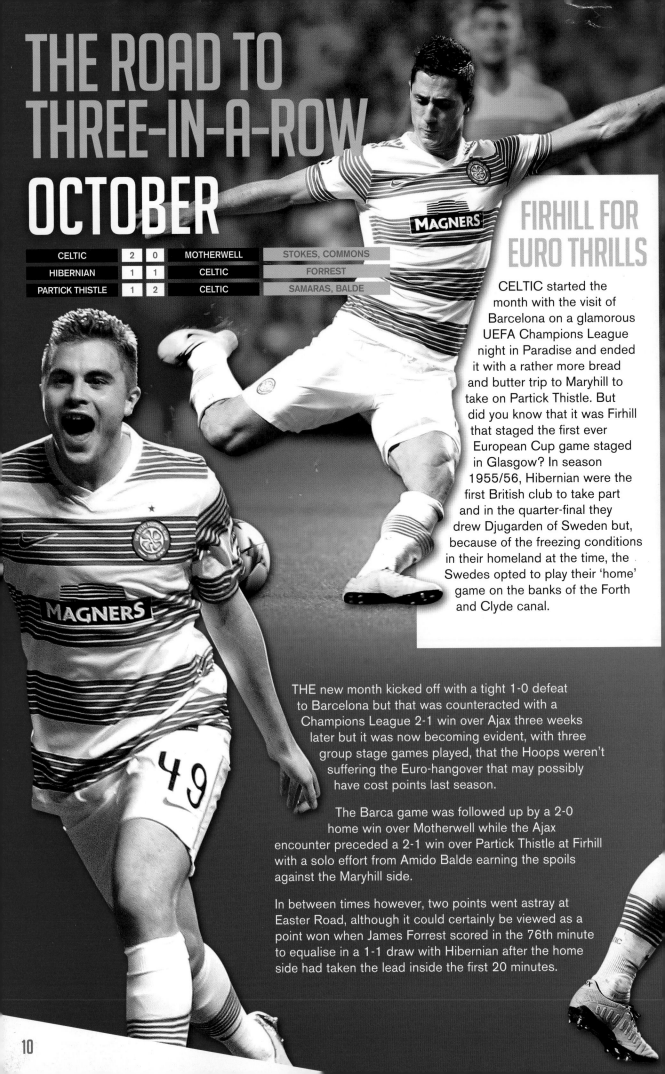

THE ROAD TO THREE-IN-A-ROW
OCTOBER

CELTIC	2	0	MOTHERWELL	STOKES, COMMONS
HIBERNIAN	1	1	CELTIC	FORREST
PARTICK THISTLE	1	2	CELTIC	SAMARAS, BALDE

FIRHILL FOR EURO THRILLS

CELTIC started the month with the visit of Barcelona on a glamorous UEFA Champions League night in Paradise and ended it with a rather more bread and butter trip to Maryhill to take on Partick Thistle. But did you know that it was Firhill that staged the first ever European Cup game staged in Glasgow? In season 1955/56, Hibernian were the first British club to take part and in the quarter-final they drew Djugarden of Sweden but, because of the freezing conditions in their homeland at the time, the Swedes opted to play their 'home' game on the banks of the Forth and Clyde canal.

THE new month kicked off with a tight 1-0 defeat to Barcelona but that was counteracted with a Champions League 2-1 win over Ajax three weeks later but it was now becoming evident, with three group stage games played, that the Hoops weren't suffering the Euro-hangover that may possibly have cost points last season.

The Barca game was followed up by a 2-0 home win over Motherwell while the Ajax encounter preceded a 2-1 win over Partick Thistle at Firhill with a solo effort from Amido Balde earning the spoils against the Maryhill side.

In between times however, two points went astray at Easter Road, although it could certainly be viewed as a point won when James Forrest scored in the 76th minute to equalise in a 1-1 draw with Hibernian after the home side had taken the lead inside the first 20 minutes.

NOVEMBER

CELTIC	1	1	DUNDEE UNITED	MULGREW
ROSS COUNTY	1	4	CELTIC	VAN DIJK 2, LEDLEY 2
CELTIC	3	1	ABERDEEN	COMMONS 2, BOERRIGTER

CELTIC went into November still unbeaten in the defence of their title but the very first game of the new month nearly threw a spanner in the works when Dundee United guarded a first-half lead until well into time added on.

A stoppage-time header from Charlie Mulgrew in the 92nd minute maintained Celtic's

unbeaten run in the SPFL but there were a couple of reverses on the European front.

Both Ajax and AC Milan inflicted defeats on the Hoops but, like in the previous month, the Celts would react in sterling style to the European games.

In between both of those matches, there were potentially tough ties against both Ross County away and Aberdeen at home in a reversal of the opening two games of the SPFL campaign.

Celtic used their heads in Dingwall with both Joe Ledley and Virgil van Dijk turning in crosses in the 4-1 win over County and, following an international break, the Dons were welcomed to Celtic Park.

Again, it was 1-1 with the seconds ticking away when two goals in the 90th minute from Derk Boerrigter and Kris Commons gave Celtic a 3-1 win.

NO ENTRY

IN the final minute of the first half against Aberdeen on November 23, former Celt Niall McGinn scored against the Hoops. It would prove to be the last league goal scored against Celtic for a very long time. Indeed, it would be the last SPFL goal scored by the opposition at Celtic Park until four months later on March 29 when Melvin de Leeuw scored for Ross County.

THE ROAD TO THREE-IN-A-ROW

DECEMBER

MOTHERWELL	0	5	CELTIC	COMMONS 2, AMBROSE, STOKES, ATAJIC
CELTIC	1	0	HIBERNIAN	PUKKI
CELTIC	2	0	HEARTS	COMMONS, FORREST
ST JOHNSTONE	0	1	CELTIC	VAN DIJK
INVERNESS CT	0	1	CELTIC	COMMONS

CELTIC'S first Friday night fixture came at the beginning of December, and the Hoops produced a superb performance at Fir Park to beat Motherwell 5-0. Kris Commons netted two, while Efe Ambrose and Anthony Stokes also scored.

And there was also a first goal from Bahrudin Atajic, while Liam Henderson also made his top-team debut at the age of 17.

Celtic returned to league action following a heavy defeat to Barcelona in the Nou Camp, and a Teemu Pukki goal was enough to give them all three points against Hibernian.

Edinburgh's other team were the next visitors to Celtic Park, and having suffered a 7-0 Scottish Cup defeat to the Hoops at Tynecastle at the beginning of the month, Hearts must have feared the worst.

They lost this league fixture, though 'only' by 2-0, with Kris Commons and James Forrest scoring the goals.

Boxing Day saw Neil Lennon's side travel through to Perth, and Virgil van Dijk scored one of the goals of the season, gathering the ball on the halfway line and then waltzing through the St Johnstone defence before firing the ball home. The goal, after just five minutes, proved to be the only one of the match.

And Celtic signed off 2013 with another 1-0 win, this time away to Inverness Caley Thistle, with Kris Commons scoring the only goal of the game after only three minutes.

GOALS GALORE

THE Hoops kick-started the month with a Scottish Cup visit to Tynecastle to take on Hearts in whirlwind fashion. The Celts really rattled the home side and conjured up a fantastic 7-0 win as they went to town in the capital. The win proved to be a record score for the Hoops against Hearts, beating the previous record of 6-0 which was achieved twice, most recently in 1981 and previously away back in 1908.

JANUARY

CELTIC	1	0	PARTICK THISTLE	LEDLEY
ST MIRREN	0	4	CELTIC	COMMONS 2, MULGREW, STOKES
CELTIC	3	0	MOTHERWELL	COMMONS 2, McMANUS OG
HIBERNIAN	0	4	CELTIC	COMMONS 2, VAN DIJK, PUKKI
CELTIC	4	0	KILMARNOCK	LEDLEY, MULGREW, BALDE, ASHCROFT OG

CELTIC kicked off 2014 with a Glasgow derby at Paradise against Partick Thistle, and on a difficult afternoon, it took a Joe Ledley goal on 39 minutes to give the Hoops all three points.

Next up was a trip to Paisley to face St Mirren, and after a goal-less first-half, Neil Lennon's side scored four second-half goals without reply. Charlie Mulgrew got the scoring underway on 53 minutes and then, five minutes later, Anthony Stokes doubled the lead.

Then Kris Commons netted a double, which also took him beyond the 50-goal milestone in the green and white Hoops.

And Commons also hit two goals in Celtic's next game - a home match against Motherwell.

The first goal came after just five minutes, and then just before half-time, he scored a second goal, this time from the penalty spot after Stokes was brought down.

With 10 minutes to go, former Celt Stephen McManus turned the ball into his own net to make it 3-0. Just minutes later, Stokes was controversially shown a straight red card for a challenge on Keith Lasley.

And the Hoops finished January with consecutive 4-0 victories. The first of those was at Easter Road, with Commons hitting two, along with goals from Teemu Pukki and a superb free-kick from Virgil van Dijk.

And the last game of January was a 4-0 win over Kilmarnock, with Charlie Mulgrew, Amido Balde and an own goal providing three of the goals, while Joe Ledley hit his last goal for the Hoops.

OWN UP

ONLY two own goals were scored for Celtic during season 2013/14 and they both came in the month of January. Indeed, they arrived in successive home league games, the first of those coming on January 18 when Motherwell visited and former Celt, Stephen McManus, inadvertently scored the third goal in a 3-0 win. Then, on January 29, Kilmarnock came calling and Lee Ashcroft was the unfortunate scorer of the second goal in a 4-0 victory.

THE ROAD TO THREE-IN-A-ROW
FEBRUARY

CELTIC	1	0	ST MIRREN		COMMONS
CELTIC	3	0	ST JOHNSTONE		STOKES 3
HEARTS	0	2	CELTIC		GRIFFITHS, PUKKI
ABERDEEN	2	1	CELTIC		FORREST

A SOLITARY Kris Commons goal after just six minutes at Celtic Park was enough to give the Hoops all three points against St Mirren. Collecting Emilio Izaguirre's pass, Commons hit an unstoppable shot from 25 yards out.

There was another Saints day at Paradise when St Johnstone were the visitors, both league games sandwiched between a shock Scottish Cup exit at the hands of Aberdeen.

Anthony Stokes hit a hat-trick against the Perth Saints to give the Hoops a comfortable 3-0 victory, which was Neil Lennon's 150th victory as Hoops boss as the champions extended their unbeaten league run this season to 25 games. And a 12th successive shut-out from Fraser Forster saw the Englishman equal Bobby Clark's Scottish top-flight clean sheet record.

A trip to Tynecastle followed, and goals from Leigh Griffiths – his first for Celtic – and Teemu Pukki gave Celtic all three points.

The last league game of February was an away game at Pittodrie, and saw the Hoops lose 2-1. Despite being down to 10 men for most of the game, Celtic were unlucky to lose the game.

And Jonny Hayes' goal in the 41st minute – which was voted Scotland's Goal of the Season – also brought to and end to Fraser Forster's sensational shut-out record.

SAFE HANDS

GOALKEEPERS may expect to receive the acclaim of the crowd when they stop a penalty or when they produce a great save in open play, but in the 31st minute the crowd in the Celtic End at Tynecastle on February 22 rose to acclaim Fraser Forster – and he was just standing in his goal. The tell-tale smile on his face gave the game away, though, he had just beaten Bobby Clark's 1,155 minute clean sheet league record. He would go on to record 1,256 minutes without losing a league goal.

MARCH

CELTIC	5	0	INVERNESS CT	GRIFFITHS 3, MULGREW, COMMONS
KILMARNOCK	0	3	CELTIC	COMMONS 3
CELTIC	3	0	ST MIRREN	JOHANSEN, GRIFFITHS, STOKES
PARTICK THISTLE	1	5	CELTIC	STOKES 2, HENDERSON, JOHANSEN, COMMONS
CELTIC	1	1	ROSS COUNTY	COMMONS

LEIGH Griffiths netted his first hat-trick for Celtic as the Champions began March in impressive style, beating Inverness Caley Thistle 5-0. Charlie Mulgrew and Kris Commons also chipped in with goals, and the Hoops headed to Rugby Park for a Friday night fixture full of confidence.

And it was Commons who took up the hat-trick mantle with three second-half strikes against a dogged Kilmarnock side. The goals confirmed Commons' importance to the team, and put Celtic a step closer to securing a third consecutive title.

Another 3-0 victory followed, this time at home to St Mirren. Stefan Johansen scored his first goal for Celtic with an impressive diving header; Griffiths and Stokes also scored.

And so Celtic headed to Firhill, knowing that victory would confirm their status as champions. And Neil Lennon's side certainly produced a performance worthy of champions.

Stokes hit a double, while Johansen made it two goals in two games, and Commons provided his customary goal.

And teenager Liam Henderson followed up an impressive performance against Kilmarnock with a sparkling second-half display at Firhill, which included his first goal in Celtic colours.

And having made it three-in-a-row, the Champions returned to Paradise, drawing 1-1 against Ross County, with Commons scoring Celtic's equaliser on the day.

NET DIFFERENCE

MELVIN de Leeuw's goal for Ross County in the 1-1 draw on March 29 meant that the Dingwall side were the only team to score in each of their league outings against Celtic during the season. The season started for Celtic with a 2-1 win over the Highland side in August and they also recorded a 4-1 win in November. St Mirren were the only side to fail to score against the Hoops with Celtic recording 4-0, 1-0 and 3-0 wins.

THE ROAD TO THREE-IN-A-ROW
APRIL

DUNDEE UNITED	0	2	CELTIC	SAMARAS, STOKES
MOTHERWELL	3	3	CELTIC	STOKES, SAMARAS, GRIFFITHS
CELTIC	6	0	INVERNESS CT	STOKES 3, GRIFFITHS, AMBROSE, PUKKI

HAVING secured the title, the Hoops began April with their final pre-split fixture – a potentially tricky trip to Tannadice. But in the event, the Champions dominated proceedings, and two goals from Georgios Samaras and Anthony Stokes gave Celtic a comfortable victory.

They followed that up with another away game, this time to Fir Park, and they found themselves two goals down against Motherwell. Stokes reduced the deficit on the stroke of half-time with a superb chip, and then goals from Samaras and Leigh Griffiths put the Hoops ahead. However, a last-gasp goal from Motherwell meant the points were shared in a 3-3 draw.

Celtic were involved in another six-goal thriller the following week against Inverness Caley Thistle, but this time all the goals were scored by the Champions.

Anthony Stokes continued his impressive scoring run with a hat-trick, while Leigh Griffiths, Teemu Pukki and Efe Ambrose also netted for the Hoops.

IF THE HAT FITS

THE triple by Anthony Stokes in the 6-0 win over Inverness Caley Thistle was his second and Celtic's sixth of the season. Georgios Samaras struck the first in a 5-2 win over Kilmarnock followed by Kris Commons doing likewise in the 7-0 win over Hearts. Stokes' first treble came in a 3-0 win over St Johnstone in February while Leigh Griffiths and Commons again, hit hat-tricks in successive wins over Inverness CT and Kilmarnock at the start of March.

MAY

CELTIC	5	2	ABERDEEN	BROWN 2, COMMONS 2, STOKES
ST JOHNSTONE	3	3	CELTIC	COMMONS, PUKKI, VAN DIJK
CELTIC	3	1	DUNDEE UNITED	STOKES, SAMARAS, COMMONS

THE first fixture of May came at Paradise, as Celtic played second-placed Aberdeen. It was a thrilling fixture with Neil Lennon's side showing their superiority to win 5-2. Both Scott Brown and Kris Commons scored two apiece, with the latter reaching an impressive 32 goals for the season, and there was also another goal for Anthony Stokes. Despite scoring three goals in their next game, the Celts only drew with St Johnstone at McDiarmid Park which meant that the 100-point tally could not be reached.

The goals from Kris Commons, Teemu Pukki and Virgil van Dijk did, however, put the Hoops on the 99-goal mark for the league, meaning the century was within their grasp.

And so it came to pass that a header from Stokes proved not only to be the 100th league goal of the season, but also the 500th competitive goal of Neil Lennon's reign as Celtic manager.

Georgios Samaras and Commons added further goals in the 3-1 win over Dundee United – a victory that proved to be the Irishman's last as manager as he announced later in the month that he was parting company with the club.

NET PROFITS

CELTIC went into the final game of the campaign knowing that they were one goal away from 100 league goals for the season but the 3-1 win also meant they had scored in every single league game of the term. Indeed, you would have to go back to December 2012 for the last league game in which Celtic failed to score – it was a 1-0 defeat to Hibernian at Easter Road.

HOLLYWOOD HOOPS

THE CELTS CHOOSE THEIR FAVOURITE FILM STARS

IN footballing terms, Celtic Park is one of the biggest and most well-known stages in the world.

Many of the greatest artistes in the world of football have trod the boards on this particular theatre of dreams, either in the green and white Hoops of Celtic or in the colours of visiting teams from all corners of the globe.

A troupe of Celtic stars more used to performing under the Paradise floodlights rather than thespian spotlights take time out to name their favourite actors or actresses.

Efe Ambrose

I like Brad Pitt. I enjoy his movies and I would like to meet him. The first one I watched was the *Legends of the Fall* and that made me like him. I have since seen a lot more films he is in. I liked *World War Z* and *Meet Joe Black* as well. I would maybe have gone for Paul Walker from the *Fast and the Furious* films, the one who died in a car crash. Those films are so good but the news about him was very sad.

Lukasz Zaluska

It's hard to choose one for myself because I watch a movie almost every day, and I go to the cinema a lot. I love movies and of course I would love to meet guys like Al Pacino and Robert De Niro but I would maybe say Gerard Butler. I met him while he was in Glasgow and he seems like a really nice lad. That would be a good option for me. I like *300* and *Law Abiding Citizen*, they were good movies. And he is a Celtic supporter too so I will go for Gerard Butler.

Anthony Stokes

Jessica Alba. I have always had a soft spot for her. I can't even remember what films she has been in but I just know she is unbelievable looking. I couldn't really care if she is a good actress or not! Like most people, I love watching Al Pacino and Robert De Niro as they are brilliant in all their films. But that's about it as I'm not that big into films.

Kris Commons

I would have to pick Robert De Niro. He's the best actor I have ever seen. I love all his movies and he's outstanding at what he does. Not only is he a serious actor, he has a good comedy aspect to him as well, with films like *Meet the Parents* which is quality. My favourite film of his is *Goodfellas*. He is immense in that. *Heat* is another classic and *Casino* is another of his top films.

BEAT BHOYS

THE SOUNDS THAT GET THE CELTS UP ON THE DANCE FLOOR

FROM *You'll Never Walk Alone* through to *Just Can't Get Enough*, the players at Celtic Park certainly hear a rundown of chart hits chorused from the stands when they strut their stuff on the hallowed turf.

But what do they listen to when they're away from their matchday residence – what are the sounds at home, in the car or on their headphones in the gym?

Here, we find out what and makes some of your heroes turn the volume up.

Adam Matthews

I'll probably say Chris Brown. He's my favourite singer at the minute, I like his style of music and he would be an interesting person to meet and speak to. He could teach me how to dance and sing while he's over as well. Would I have a sing-off with him? I think he'd beat me but I'd give it a go.

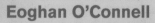

Eoghan O'Connell

Paolo Nutini – I'm a big fan of his. He seems quite funny and comes across as a good guy. I'd probably make him get up and sing if he was there as well, I'm sure he'd be fine with that. He's a Celtic fan as well actually. I like his music and he seems like a cool guy so he'd be a good one to meet.

Teemu Pukki

Justin Timberlake. I like his music and he was over in Finland during the summer but we were involved in pre-season training. I don't think he has been to Finland before. He is also a good actor, I have liked watching him in his films - he seems like a really funny guy. Maybe if I invite him he will sing some songs for us as well.

Mikael Lustig

I will go for the Swedish House Mafia. I'm not a big fan but they have some decent songs and seem like pretty cool guys. They have been really big back home, maybe more so in the last year than before that, but they are massive in America. It took them a while to be big in Sweden but in the last couple of years everyone seems to know who they are, but then they split up of course.

Beram Kayal

Beyonce. When I came to the UK I started taking an interest in British and American music and she has been at the top over the last few years. She is brilliant. It's not just her singing, it's the way she dances as well – she puts on a show. She is nice and has a very nice voice. I like her. I would like to go and see her in concert but haven't seen her yet. I like a few musicians back home as well but the names aren't famous outside of Israel, like Beyonce.

SPOT THE DIFFERENCE

THERE are 12 differences between these pictures of Scott Brown in action in against Aberdeen. The first one has been circled, but can you spot the rest?

Answers on pages 62/63.

SPFL SEASON 2013/14 QUIZ

01	Who scored Celtic's first goal of the campaign?
02	How many goals did Celtic score during the march to the title?
03	Against which side did Lukasz Zaluska keep goal?
04	Which side did Fraser Forster's clean sheet run begin against?
05	Charlie Mulgrew scored an injury-time winner against which side?
06	Celtic's final two games were against the Scottish Cup finalists – who were they?
07	The Hoops won their final game of 2013 and their first game of 2014 by the same scoreline – what was it?
08	How many games did Fraser Forster go without losing a goal to create a new record?
09	Against which side did Celtic clinch the title?
10	Which Celt scored the last goal of the campaign?

How did you do? Find out with the answers on pages 62/63.

BILLY McNEILL
OUT AT THE TOP

EXIT

There was only one way for Cesar to go out and that was at the top. He announced his retirement from playing immediately after lifting the Scottish Cup in the 1975 final. Paul Wilson scored two first-half goals and Pat McCluskey scored from the spot after the break in a 3-1 win over Airdrie in front of a crowd of 75,457. He had stopped as a winner but, at the age of 35 – he later admitted that he probably retired too early.

POSTER BHOYS

WHO DID THE CELTS LOOK UP TO WHEN THEY WERE YOUNGER?

WE all have our favourite Celts and we all have our favourite players from around the world, but who are the heroes of the men who play in the green and white?

Here are four Celts here telling us just who influenced them as young players trying to make their way through the grades.

Adam Matthews

I'd have to say Steven Gerrard. Being a Liverpool fan I've grown up watching him and he's been their best player over the last 10 years. I like the way he plays, and I think he is a great role model for every young footballer so it would be interesting to speak to him and see what he has to say. I played against him in Dublin and that was a bit weird. When we were in the tunnel I think I was just staring at him. It was a great experience though and at least now I can say I have played against him, even if it was just a friendly. I asked for his shirt but Fraser Forster already had it.

John Herron

I would say Zinedine Zidane as I watched him a lot when I was younger with him being a midfielder like me. He scored a lot of great goals for Real Madrid and he drove at teams and his goal at Hampden just topped it off. At the moment, my favourite player is Xavi so I would like to bring him as well and hopefully get a few tips. It would be a good dinner table to have him and Zidane there.

Efe Ambrose

Ronaldo (de Lima), he is my football idol because there is no one like him. I saw him playing in the Olympics and the World Cup. When I was growing up I got to know how he played – his movement, his pace, what he does with the ball, and there's no one like him. I liked playing up front like him when I was younger, in attack, and scoring goals. I would've liked to come up against Brazil in the World Cup this year because I've supported them because of him, but obviously if that happened I would've been supporting my country instead.

Mikael Lustig

It would probably have to be Allesandro Del Piero who played for Juventus. He was probably my first real idol and I liked him because I played as a striker from a young age. I moved back to defence when I started playing first-team football at senior level though. I really liked Italian football as well and supported Juventus. I have never met him but I have seen him play live a couple of times.

MAZE

THE SPFL trophy had to make its way from the Celtic Park trophy room down to the pitch for the Championship presentation.

Can you help us out by taking the silverware from the heart of the stadium down to the hallowed turf?

Find out how the trophy made its way through Paradise on pages 62/63.

QUIZ QUESTIONS

01	In which city did Celtic kick-off their 2013/14 European campaign?
02	Which two Celts played in every single league game?
03	How many times have Celtic won the league?
04	Celtic's four final league opponents were connected in what way?
05	The Hoops played four home games in a row during 2013/14 – who against?

Check out the answers on pages 62/63.

WORDSEARCH

01	Celtic's Norwegian midfielder.
02	The Hoops' training ground.
03	We are the…
04	The national side of Efe Ambrose.
05	Home base of Leigh Griffith's former club.
06	Home country of Virgil van Dijk.
07	Fraser Forster had loads of these.
08	Our Welsh defender.
09	We beat them in the European Cup final.

Answers on pages 62/63

A	S	P	I	R	D	A	H	J	V	S	S	C
B	C	T	H	N	I	P	O	W	D	Q	W	H
B	E	O	U	R	T	H	H	N	Z	B	E	A
C	K	T	E	O	A	E	A	W	W	W	H	M
L	Q	G	D	N	T	L	R	W	K	D	T	P
S	I	Z	S	R	R	U	T	M	W	N	T	I
N	D	E	I	E	L	B	H	V	I	K	A	O
F	N	J	H	J	N	N	J	S	V	L	M	N
G	H	T	X	U	E	N	I	L	O	M	A	S
M	E	Q	W	Z	H	V	O	C	H	T	D	N
N	W	B	P	J	Z	L	P	H	W	F	D	C
B	Y	L	X	S	A	F	D	U	X	Q	S	U
L	E	N	N	O	X	T	O	W	N	Y	S	E

PAT BONNER
OUT AT THE TOP

EXIT

After initially leaving the club, his return, thanks to the intervention of Tommy Burns, delivered another 25 appearances for the keeper. Those extra games not only brought him up level with Alec McNair in the appearance charts, but also presented him with the opportunity to go out on a high. It restarted for real on Boxing Day, 1995 when he took over the No.1 position from Gordon Marshall. He maintained his place for every single game except the Scottish Cup fourth-round win over Meadowbank Thistle. This meant he was between the sticks for the final on May 27 when a Pierre van Hooijdonk goal against Airdrie delivered Celtic's first silverware since 1999.

PARADISE PENPIX

THE CELTIC FOOTBALL CLUB · 1888

SCOTT BROWN	DYLAN MCGEOUCH	JACKSON IRVINE	EOGHAN O'CONNELL
LUKASZ ZALUSKA	FILIP TWARDZIK	AMIDO BALDE	DARNELL FISHER
JAMES FORREST	MARCUS FRASER	VIRGIL VAN DIJK	CALLUM MCGREGOR
BERAM KAYAL	MIKAEL LUSTIG	DERK BOERRIGTER	LIAM HENDERSON
CHARLIE MULGREW	PAUL GEORGE	NIR BITTON	CRAIG GORDON
EMILIO IZAGUIRRE	TOM ROGIC	TEEMU PUKKI	JASON DENAYER
KRIS COMMONS	EFE AMBROSE	HOLMBERT FRIDJONSSON	JO INGE BERGET
ANTHONY STOKES	JOE CHALMERS	STEFAN JOHANSEN	ALEKSANDAR TONEV
ADAM MATTHEWS	JOHN HERRON	LEIGH GRIFFITHS	

SCOTT BROWN

POSITION: MIDFIELDER

D.O.B.: 25/06/85

HEIGHT: 5'10"

DEBUT: V KILMARNOCK (H) 0-0 (SPL) 05/08/07

SQUAD NUMBER: 8

BORN: HILL O' BEATH SCOTLAND

SIGNED: 29/05/07

PREVIOUS CLUBS: HIBERNIAN YOUTH

POSITION: DEFENDER

D.O.B.: 28/06/95

HEIGHT: 6'0"

DEBUT: V DUNDEE UNITED (H) 6-1 (SPFL) 16/08/14

SQUAD NUMBER: 22

BORN: BRUSSELS BELGIUM

SIGNED: 11/08/14 ON LOAN

PREVIOUS CLUBS: MANCHESTER CITY YOUTH, JMG ACADEMY YOUTH, RSC ANDERLECHT YOUTH, FC GANSHOREN YOUTH

JASON DENAYER

LUKASZ ZALUSKA

POSITION	GOALKEEPER 
D.O.B.	 16/06/82
HEIGHT	 6'4"
DEBUT	 V FALKIRK (A) 4-0 (LC) 23/09/09
SQUAD NUMBER	24
BORN	WYSOKIE MAZOWIECKIE POLAND 
SIGNED	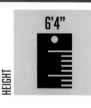 01/06/09
PREVIOUS CLUBS	DUNDEE UNITED, KORONA KIELCE, LEGIA WARSAW, STOMIL OLSZTYN, ZRYW ZIELONA GORA, SPARTA OBORNOKI, MSP SZAMOTULY, RUCH WYSOKIE MAZOWIECKIE YOUTH, JAGIELLONIA BIALYSTOK (LOAN)

JAMES FORREST

POSITION	ATTACKER 
D.O.B.	 07/07/91
HEIGHT	 5'9"
DEBUT	V MOTHERWELL (H) 4-0 (SPL) 01/05/10
SQUAD NUMBER	 49
BORN	GLASGOW SCOTLAND
SIGNED	 30/08/09
PREVIOUS CLUBS	CELTIC YOUTH

BERAM KAYAL

POSITION	MIDFIELDER 
D.O.B.	 02/05/88
HEIGHT	5'10"
DEBUT	 V FC UTRECHT (H) 2-0 (EL) 19/08/10
SQUAD NUMBER	 33
BORN	JADEIDI ISRAEL 
SIGNED	29/07/10
PREVIOUS CLUBS	MACCABI HAIFA, MACCABI HAIFA YOUTH

CHARLIE MULGREW

POSITION	DEFENDER 
D.O.B.	 06/03/86
HEIGHT	 6'2"
DEBUT	 V SC BRAGA (A) 0-3 (UCL) 28/07/10
SQUAD NUMBER	 21
BORN	GLASGOW SCOTLAND
SIGNED	 01/07/10
PREVIOUS CLUBS	ABERDEEN, SOUTHEND UNITED (LOAN), WOLVERHAMPTON WANDERERS, DUNDEE UNITED (LOAN), CELTIC YOUTH 

PARADISE PENPIX

EMILIO IZAGUIRRE

POSITION: DEFENDER

D.O.B.: 10/05/86

HEIGHT: 5'8"

DEBUT: V MOTHERWELL (A) 1-0 (SPL) 29/08/10

SQUAD NUMBER: 3

BORN: TEGUCIGALPA HONDURAS

SIGNED: 18/08/10

PREVIOUS CLUBS: MOTAGUA

KRIS COMMONS

POSITION: MIDFIELDER

D.O.B.: 30/08/83

HEIGHT: 5'6"

DEBUT: V ABERDEEN (H) 4-1 (CIS) 29/01/11

SQUAD NUMBER: 15

BORN: MANSFIELD ENGLAND

SIGNED: 18/08/10

PREVIOUS CLUBS: DERBY COUNTY, NOTTINGHAM FOREST, STOKE CITY, STOKE CITY YOUTH

ANTHONY STOKES

POSITION: ATTACKER

D.O.B.: 25/07/88

HEIGHT: 5'11"

DEBUT: V HEARTS (H) 3-0 (SPL) 11/09/11

SQUAD NUMBER: 10

BORN: DUBLIN IRELAND

SIGNED: 31/08/10

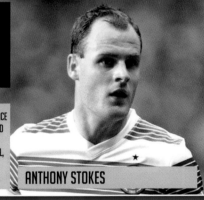

PREVIOUS CLUBS: HIBERNIAN, CRYSTAL PALACE (LOAN), SHEFFIELD UNITED (LOAN), SUNDERLAND, FALKIRK (LOAN), ARSENAL, ARSENAL YOUTH, SHELBOURNE YOUTH

ADAM MATTHEWS

POSITION: DEFENDER

D.O.B.: 13/01/92

HEIGHT: 5'10"

DEBUT: V ABERDEEN (A) 1-0 (SPL) 07/08/11

SQUAD NUMBER: 2

BORN: SWANSEA WALES

SIGNED: 01/07/11

PREVIOUS CLUBS: CARDIFF CITY, CARDIFF CITY YOUTH

DYLAN McGEOUCH

POSITION	D.O.B.	HEIGHT	DEBUT
MIDFIELDER	15/01/93	5'10"	V MOTHERWELL (A) 2-1 (SPL) 06/11/11

  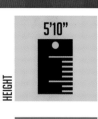 

SQUAD NUMBER	BORN	SIGNED	PREVIOUS CLUBS
46	GLASGOW SCOTLAND	01/06/11	CELTIC YOUTH, RANGERS YOUTH

FILIP TWARDZIK

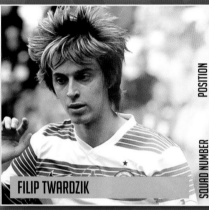

POSITION	D.O.B.	HEIGHT	DEBUT
MIDFIELDER	10/02/93	6'2"	V PETERHEAD (A) 3-0 (SC) 08/01/12

SQUAD NUMBER	BORN	SIGNED	PREVIOUS CLUBS
56	TRINEC CZECH REPUBLIC	31/01/09	HERTHA BSC YOUTH, SACHSEN LEIPZIG YOUTH, CELTIC YOUTH

JO INGE BERGET

POSITION	D.O.B.	HEIGHT	DEBUT
MIDFIELDER	11/09/90	6'0"	V LEGIA WARSAW (A) 1-4 (UCL) 30/07/14

SQUAD NUMBER	BORN	SIGNED	PREVIOUS CLUBS
16	HADELAND NORWAY	28/07/014 ON LOAN	CARDIFF CITY, MOLDE, STROMSGODSET (LOAN), LYN (LOAN), UDINESE, LYN YOUTH

MARCUS FRASER

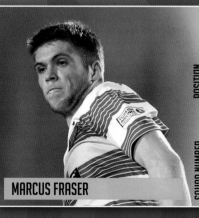

POSITION	D.O.B.	HEIGHT	DEBUT
DEFENDER	23/06/94	5'11"	V RENNES (H) 3-1 (EL) 03/11/11

SQUAD NUMBER	BORN	SIGNED	PREVIOUS CLUBS
44	BISHOPBRIGGS SCOTLAND	01/08/10	CELTIC YOUTH

PARADISE PENPIX

MIKAEL LUSTIG

POSITION	DEFENDER 
D.O.B.	13/12/86
HEIGHT	6'2" 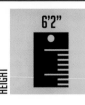
DEBUT	V ABERDEEN (A) 1-1 (SPL) 03/03/12 
SQUAD NUMBER	23 
BORN	UMEA SWEDEN 
SIGNED	01/01/12
PREVIOUS CLUBS	ROSENBORG, GIF SUNDSVALL, UMEA, SANDAKERMS SK

PAUL GEORGE

POSITION	ATTACKER
D.O.B.	27/01/94
HEIGHT	5'9"
DEBUT	V ROSS COUNTY (A) 2-0 (LC) 21/11/11 
SQUAD NUMBER	50 
BORN	KILLOUGH IRELAND 
SIGNED	01/08/11 
PREVIOUS CLUBS	CELTIC YOUTH

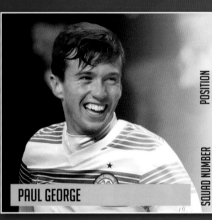

EFE AMBROSE

POSITION	DEFENDER 
D.O.B.	18/10/88
HEIGHT	6'3" 
DEBUT	V DUNDEE (H) 2-0 (SPL) 22/09/12
SQUAD NUMBER	4 
BORN	KADUNA NIGERIA 
SIGNED	31/08/12 
PREVIOUS CLUBS	FC ASHDOD, KADUNA UNITED, BAYELSA UNITED (LOAN)

TOM ROGIC

POSITION	MIDFIELDER
D.O.B.	 16/12/92
HEIGHT	6'2" 
DEBUT	V INVERNESS CT (A) 3-1 (SPL) 09/02/13 
SQUAD NUMBER	18
BORN	GRIFFITH AUSTRALIA
SIGNED	17/01/13 
PREVIOUS CLUBS	CENTRAL COAST MARINERS, BELCONNEN UNITED, ANU FC, NIKE FOOTBALL ACADEMY YOUTH, TUGGERANONG UNITED YOUTH

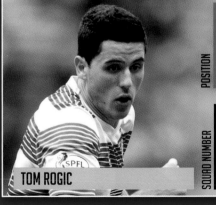

JOHN HERRON

POSITION	MIDFIELDER
D.O.B.	01/02/94
HEIGHT	6'0"
DEBUT	V ROSS COUNTY (H) 4-0 (SPL) 22/12/12
SQUAD NUMBER	31
BORN	COATBRIDGE SCOTLAND
SIGNED	12/07/10
PREVIOUS CLUBS	CELTIC YOUTH

JOE CHALMERS

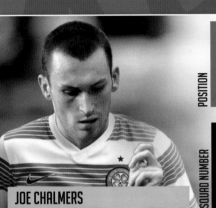

POSITION	DEFENDER
D.O.B.	03/01/94
HEIGHT	6'1"
DEBUT	V INVERNESS CT (A) 4-2 (SPL) 25/08/12
SQUAD NUMBER	43
BORN	RUTHERGLEN SCOTLAND
SIGNED	12/07/10
PREVIOUS CLUBS	CELTIC YOUTH

AMIDO BALDE

POSITION	ATTACKER
D.O.B.	16/05/91
HEIGHT	6'4"
DEBUT	V CLIFTONVILLE (H), 2-0 (UCL), 23/07/13
SQUAD NUMBER	17
BORN	BISSAU GUINEA-BISSAU
SIGNED	13/06/13
PREVIOUS CLUBS	VITORIA GUIMARAES, CERCLE BRUGGE (LOAN), BADAJOZ (LOAN), SANTA CLARA (LOAN), SPORTING LISBON, SPORTING BISSAU YOUTH

JACKSON IRVINE

POSITION	MIDFIELDER
D.O.B.	07/03/93
HEIGHT	6'2"
DEBUT	V HIBERNIAN (H) 2-2 (SPL) 01/09/12
SQUAD NUMBER	36
BORN	MELBOURNE, AUSTRALIA
SIGNED	19/11/10
PREVIOUS CLUBS	KILMARNOCK, CELTIC, FRANKSTON PINES, CELTIC YOUTH, MELBOURNE VICTORY YOUTH, RICHMOND SC YOUTH, ENDEAVOUR UNITED YOUTH, KNOX CITY YOUTH

PARADISE PENPIX

DERK BOERRIGTER

POSITION	ATTACKER
D.O.B.	16/10/86
HEIGHT	6'2" 
DEBUT	V ROSS COUNTY (H) 2-1 (SPFL) 03/08/13
SQUAD NUMBER	11 
BORN	OLDENZAAL NETHERLANDS
SIGNED	30/07/13
PREVIOUS CLUBS	AJAX, RKC WAALWIJK, HAARLEM (LOAN), AJAX

VIRGIL VAN DIJK

POSITION	DEFENDER 
D.O.B.	08/07/91 
HEIGHT	6'4" 
DEBUT	V ABERDEEN (A) 2-0 (SPFL) 17/08/13 
SQUAD NUMBER	5
BORN	BREDA NETHERLANDS
SIGNED	21/06/13
PREVIOUS CLUBS	GRONINGEN, GRONINGEN YOUTH, WILLEM II YOUTH

TEEMU PUKKI

POSITION	ATTACKER
D.O.B.	29/03/90 
HEIGHT	5'11" 
DEBUT	V HEARTS (A) 3-1 (SPFL) 14/09/13 
SQUAD NUMBER	20
BORN	KOTKA FINLAND
SIGNED	31/08/13
PREVIOUS CLUBS	SCHALKE 04, HJK, SEVILLA, SEVILLA ATLETICO, FC KOOTEEPEE, FC KOOTEEPEE YOUTH'

NIR BITTON

POSITION	MIDFIELDER 
D.O.B.	30/10/91 
HEIGHT	6'5"
DEBUT	V AC MILAN (A) 0-2 (UCL) 18/09/13
SQUAD NUMBER	6 
BORN	ASHDOD ISRAEL 
SIGNED	30/08/13
PREVIOUS CLUBS	FC ASHDOD, FC ASHDOD YOUTH 

LEIGH GRIFFITHS

POSITION	ATTACKER 
D.O.B.	 20/08/90
HEIGHT	5'8"
DEBUT	V ABERDEEN (H) 1-2 (SC) 08/02/14
SQUAD NUMBER	28
BORN	EDINBURGH SCOTLAND 
SIGNED	31/01/14
PREVIOUS CLUBS	WOLVERHAMPTON WANDERERS, HIBERNIAN (LOAN), DUNDEE, LIVINGSTON, FALKIRK YOUTH, HIBERNIAN YOUTH

HOLMBERT FRIDJONSSON

POSITION	ATTACKER 
D.O.B.	 19/04/93
HEIGHT	6'5" 
DEBUT	N/A 
SQUAD NUMBER	19
BORN	REYKJAVIK ICELAND 
SIGNED	01/01/14
PREVIOUS CLUBS	FRAM REYKJAVIK, HK KÓPAVOGS

DARNELL FISHER

POSITION	DEFENDER
D.O.B.	 04/04/94
HEIGHT	5'9" 
DEBUT	V HIBERNIAN (A) 1-1 (SPFL) 19/10/13 
SQUAD NUMBER	41
BORN	READING ENGLAND 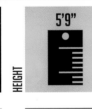
SIGNED	01/07/12 
PREVIOUS CLUBS	CELTIC YOUTH, FARNBOROUGH YOUTH

STEFAN JOHANSEN

POSITION	MIDFIELDER
D.O.B.	 08/01/91
HEIGHT	5'11" 
DEBUT	V HIBERNIAN (A) 4-0 (SPFL) 26/01/14
SQUAD NUMBER	25
BORN	VARDO NORWAY 
SIGNED	15/01/14 
PREVIOUS CLUBS	STROMSGODSET, BODO/GLIMT

PARADISE PENPIX

LIAM HENDERSON

- **POSITION:** MIDFIELDER
- **D.O.B.:** 25/04/96
- **HEIGHT:** 6'0"
- **DEBUT:** V MOTHERWELL (A) 5-0 (SPFL) 06/12/13
- **SQUAD NUMBER:** 53
- **BORN:** LIVINGSTON SCOTLAND
- **SIGNED:** 01/07/13
- **PREVIOUS CLUBS:** CELTIC YOUTH, HEARTS YOUTH

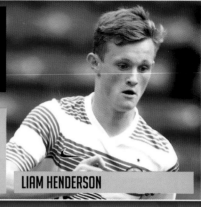

EOGHAN O'CONNELL

- **POSITION:** DEFENDER
- **D.O.B.:** 13/08/95
- **HEIGHT:** 6'2"
- **DEBUT:** V ROSS COUNTY (H) 1-1 (SPFL) 29/03/14
- **SQUAD NUMBER:** 34
- **BORN:** CORK IRELAND
- **SIGNED:** 01/07/13
- **PREVIOUS CLUBS:** CELTIC YOUTH

CRAIG GORDON

- **POSITION:** GOALKEEPER
- **D.O.B.:** 31/12/82
- **HEIGHT:** 6'4"
- **DEBUT:** V ST JOHNSTONE (A) 3-0 (SPFL) 13/08/14
- **SQUAD NUMBER:** 26
- **BORN:** EDINBURGH SCOTLAND
- **SIGNED:** 03/07/14
- **PREVIOUS CLUBS:** SUNDERLAND, HEARTS, COWDENBEATH (LOAN)

CALLUM McGREGOR

- **POSITION:** MIDFIELDER
- **D.O.B.:** 14/06/93
- **HEIGHT:** 5'9"
- **DEBUT:** V KR REYKJAVIK (A) 1-0 (UCL) 15/07/14
- **SQUAD NUMBER:** 42
- **BORN:** GLASGOW SCOTLAND
- **SIGNED:** 01/08/11
- **PREVIOUS CLUBS:** NOTTS COUNTY (LOAN) CELTIC YOUTH

ALEKSANDAR TONEV

POSITION

ATTACKER

D.O.B.

03/02/90

HEIGHT

5'10"

DEBUT

V DYNAMO DRESDEN
(A) 1-1
19/07/14

SQUAD NUMBER

27

BORN

ELIN PELIN
BULGARIA

SIGNED

11/08/14
ON LOAN

PREVIOUS CLUBS

ASTON VILLA,
LECH POZNAN,
SLIVEN (LOAN),
CSKA SOFIA

GUESS THE GUEST
WHO'S WHO AT THE DINNER TABLE?

WE HAVE FOUR CELTS HERE AND THEIR FOUR IDEAL DINNER GUESTS FROM ALL TIME, BUT WE'VE GOT THE DINNER INVITATIONS JUMBLED UP AND WE DON'T KNOW WHICH PLAYER HAS INVITED WHICH DINER.

The Hoops are Kris Commons, Efe Ambrose, Anthony Stokes and John Herron and the ideal invites would be Rafa Nadal, Nelson Mandela, Michael Jordan and Muhammad Ali – but can you guess who will be sitting at whose dinner table?

See how many you can guess correctly - the answers are on pages 62/63, good luck.

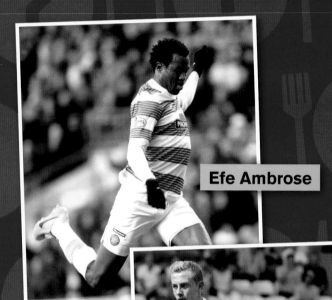

Efe Ambrose

Anthony Stokes

John Herron

Kris Commons

This is a tough one as there are a lot of people I would like to meet. I would maybe go for someone like Nelson Mandela just because of what he had been through in his life and I just think he would have a better insight into life than 99 per cent of people. There are a lot of people I would like to meet for the sake of meeting them, but I would probably have gone for him. I haven't read too much about him, but I know about what he went through in his life in prison and then after he came out. The biggest thing about him, though, is that he touched so many people and how he changed things in South Africa.

Nelson Mandela

Rafa Nadal

I think I will go for Rafa Nadal because he is my favourite tennis player. I like tennis a lot. I don't play it but I like playing table tennis, and that's similar so that's why I enjoy watching tennis on the television. He doesn't give up as he always wants to win and has a good mentality. He's always giving his best in matches and comes across as a nice guy as well. I would invite him to see if his personality is really that good.

Michael Jordan

One person I would like to sit down with is Michael Jordan. I have been watching a lot of basketball recently, especially with the finals being on towards the end of June. I find him breathtaking. I have watched so much footage of him recently of what he did in his career and how he changed the game. With all the basketball on TV, everyone has been debating whether LeBron James or Kobe Bryant are the best in the world but everyone always brings up Michael Jordan so I decided to do some research on him and I've read a lot about him. He would be a great one to sit down and have a bite to eat with.

Muhammad Ali

I would definitely say Muhammad Ali as I like boxing a lot and when I was younger I did a bit of boxing and stuff. I watched a lot of him growing up as well. He would probably have a lot of good stories and would be quite funny so I would probably bring him.

ON ME PLATE SON

THE IDEAL MEAL – AS PREPARED BY THE PLAYERS

FOOD & DRINK MENU

THE Celts have certainly served us up a tasty morsel or so when it comes to dishing out defeats to opposition teams after experiencing some of the best pre-match meals in the business.

Pre-match meals, however, aren't on the menu when the players invite someone around for dinner so here are a few dishes that may be on the table in the homes of your heroes.

FOOD & DRINK MENU

Beram Kayal

The best meal for me is sushi. I have it once a week or once every two weeks. My family also like it so we have that at a restaurant if we go out. So if you asked me to have something it would be sushi.

Efe Ambrose

I prefer my wife cooking for me so I'd get her to make us dinner. I can cook but she always does it because she is better. I enjoy rice, tomato sauce and chicken so I would serve that to my guests.

FOOD & DRINK
MENU

Mikael Lustig

That would have to be pancakes. That was my favourite meal when I was younger – it maybe still is. I like them small and thin and I would have jam and cream on them.

John Herron

I can't cook one thing! If I am ever up at my girlfriend's she is always saying, 'any chance of you cooking!' So I would need to bring my girlfriend over as she is a good cook as the only thing I can cook is something in the microwave…I would have to settle for beans on toast outside that!

FOOD & DRINK
MENU

Eoghan O'Connell

Depends what night it is – if it's a Saturday I'd call in a Chinese. Do I have to cook? Surely I don't have to cook? I'm not the best cook, I've never really tried it so I'd go for a chicken curry and get my mum on the phone. She could talk me through it.

Anthony Stokes

The only decent meal that I can cook is steak and chips! That's about it from me. My missus does the rest of the cooking in the house. That's my meal – a big fillet steak, some chips and a bit of gravy. Other than that, I will just order Italian food – spaghetti or garlic bread.

PLAYERS' PAST PASTIMES...

WE'RE sure you all love playing football as well as watching it when Celtic take to the field, but we are also sure that you have many other hobbies and interests and take part in other sports whether at school or with your friends.

But, other than football, what were the other sports that your Celtic favourites played when they were kids?

Are they the same as yours? Well, we all like to keep fit so we asked some of the Hoops players what sports they played away from football when they were younger.

Holmbert Fridjonsson

I played handball for a few years as it's a big sport in Iceland. I was a goalkeeper and I was alright at it. All my friends played it and it was fun. I played that for quite a while – five or six years. When I signed my contract with HK at 16, I could only play football and had to quit. I had to choose between handball and football but it was always going to be football. Two of my best friends still play handball at the best level in Iceland.

James Forrest

I played tennis. You know what it's like growing up, you will play any sport that is going so I played a bit of that. There were tennis courts around the corner from where I lived and that is why I played it a lot. I was okay but then I got to around 14/15 and decided to stop playing and concentrate on football. My best shot? I was an all-rounder. I haven't played it in a couple of years now.

Teemu Pukki

I liked to play all kinds of sports but I never joined any team or went to their practice, it was only football. I liked basketball and ice hockey which used to be fun to play in the winter outside with your friends. It's a big thing in Finland but I never liked it as much as football.

Nir Bitton

During the close season holiday, I liked playing tennis and basketball. I played a lot of tennis with my friends. I tried to forget about football for this month and just work on my body, and enjoy tennis and basketball. I just liked playing them and sometimes I prefer to watch basketball rather than football. The best team in Israel are one of the most successful teams in Europe – Maccabi Tel Aviv. They are like the team of the country and most of the people support them. Last year, I went to about 80 per cent of their games. There is a great atmosphere – I really like watching basketball.

GLASGOW BELONGS TO US

CELTIC YOUTH ACADEMY BHOYS LIFT HISTORIC TROPHY ON THE WAY TO CLINCHING A TREBLE.

THE Glasgow Cup returned to Paradise for the first time in three years as Celtic Under-17s deservedly defeated their city rivals Rangers 1-0 in the final on their way to a terrific treble.

Aidan Nesbitt was the hero for the Tommy McIntyre's young guns, firing home the only goal of the game with only 17 minutes remaining on the clock.

Having dominated the match and impressed with their adventurous, passing brand of football it was a thoroughly-merited triumph for the Bhoys.

They had come within inches of taking the lead in the first half when Regan Hendry's ferocious shot from distance cannoned off the inside of the post.

But that only proved a reprieve for the Ibrox side as Nesbitt capped off a polished performance with a clinical finish into the far corner at the second attempt after his first effort had been blocked.

And there were memorable scenes following the final whistle as captain Joe Thomson lifted the historic trophy aloft in Celtic Park and the youngsters and coaching staff celebrated their success with the watching Hoops support.

That sealed the double for the young Celts after they had lifted the SPFL U19 league title earlier in the season, despite facing more experienced opponents throughout the campaign.

They got their hands on the prize following a 1-0 away victory over Queen's Park in mid-December, with Fiacre Kelleher heading home the decisive goal.

And it rounded off an excellent campaign from the youths, who scored 43 goals in 13 games and only conceded nine as they dominated the championship from start to finish.

Now also in possession of the City of Glasgow Cup, the young Hoops had put themselves in a position to make a clean sweep of trophies, with the U19 League Cup still up for grabs.

A 5-2 semi-final triumph over Arbroath in May booked their place in the showpiece event against Ayr United at their home ground – Somerset Park.

Denied the services of seven players, who were representing Scotland U17s in The UEFA European Championship in Malta, the Bhoys nonetheless battled gamely and opened the scoring through Ciaran Lafferty's fine header in the 64th minute.

However, Ayr fought back and forced extra time when Ryan Nisbet's low effort found the net, sending the game into extra time.

Recovering quickly from that setback, though, Luke Donnelly's clever turn and finish at the start of the additional 30 minutes saw the young Hoops clinch a hat-trick of trophies to end a sensational season with a flourish.

COLOUR ME IN

STEFAN Johansen picks up the ball in midfield here and we want you to get out your crayons, ink markers or paints and bring this image to full Celtic technicolour.

GUESS WHO?

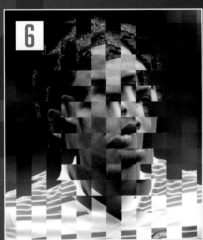

Answers on pages 62/63.

JACKIE McNAMARA

EXIT

OUT AT THE TOP

The 2005 Scottish Cup final against Dundee United provided the setting for McNamara's last competitive start for Celtic. Less than a week had elapsed since the disappointing events at Fir Park and the hurt of losing the league remained raw. Nonetheless, the Hoops had to rouse themselves for the game and try to end the campaign with at least one piece of silverware to show for their efforts. And they managed to achieve a degree of redemption. Alan Thompson's 11th minute strike settled the final, allowing McNamara to lead his team up the Hampden steps and lift his first trophy as captain. It was a happy ending to his Celtic career, although he wouldn't know that at the time.

CELTS OF THE YEAR

★ ★ ★ ★ ★

AWARDS CEREMONY SUITS THE HOOPS

IT was Kris Commons who lifted Celtic's Player of the Year trophy for season 2013/14. The award, voted for by the fans, was presented to him just 24 hours after reaching the 30-goal mark with a double in the 5-2 victory over Aberdeen.

The Players' Player of the Year award was a close-run contest, with Fraser Forster and Virgil van Dijk sharing the award after all the players' votes had been counted up.

It was a tough choice for supporters to choose their Goal of the Season. The Champions scored so many great goals

during the season but a shortlist of 10 was finally agreed upon.

And from that, it was Kris Commons with his second award of the night who won for his brilliant strike against Shakhter Karagandy in the UEFA Champions League qualifier, a goal which helped Celtic reach the group stages of the competition for the second season in a row.

And with an impressive 32 goals to his name for the season, Commons also lifted the Top Goalscorer of the Season.

It was a good season for Celtic's Youth Academy with a number of young players promoted to the first-team squad. Darnell Fisher, who made 13 first-team appearances, was named Young Player of the Year.

And Liam Henderson, who broke into the top team in the last few months of the season lifted a new award – the Academy Player of the Year.

FOOTBALL FIRSTS

THERE'S nothing like the thrill of scoring a goal, but can you remember the first goals you scored?
That's just one of the questions we asked this Celtic quartet to find out some of their earliest football memories.

HOLMBERT FRIDJONSSON

First goal

I remember scoring a free-kick when I was about 13 or 14 for HK. I used to take free-kicks for my old clubs. That one just sticks out.

First strip

A Liverpool one, I must have been around six or seven. My Dad was a Liverpool fan and I was one as well. I didn't have a number on the back but I think I got 'OWEN' on it.

First silverware

Probably when I was 10 and won a cup. At the end of a season, the club also had individual awards for every age-group and I won the Most Promising Player award.

NIR BITTON

First goal

It was in a cup game in Israel and it was my debut. It was the day before I turned 17. I came on in the 73rd minute and I scored a goal in the 75th minute. It is something I will never forget. The striker ran down the right with the ball and it was a two versus one. I ran in behind and he gave me the ball. I took one touch with my left and put it inside the post. It was against one of the best teams in Israel as well, Maccabi Tel Aviv. It was unbelievable.

First strip

Maybe Real Madrid. When I was a child, I liked Madrid and I may have been about six or seven when I had the strip.

First silverware

I was 17 and I played with the Under-20 side and we won one of the national cups so that was my first trophy.

TEEMU PUKKI

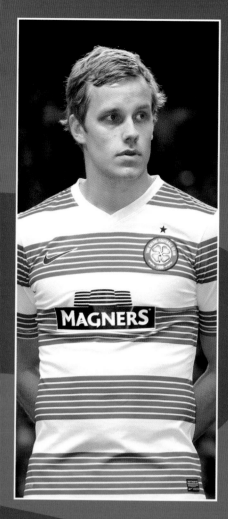

First goal

It was a tournament when I was about 10 or 11 and it was the biggest tournament you could play in at that age. We got to the final and first of all I missed a penalty. But then two minutes later I got the ball from the left, cut inside and then scored with a shot from around 15 yards.

First strip

My Grandmother always travelled when I was younger and used to bring me some shirts back. It might have been a strip from Spain – Real Madrid or Barcelona. I had them both so I can't remember what one was first. When I was 12 or 13, I played in a tournament in Barcelona and we went to see a game there and it was a good one, ending 4-4 and Litmanen was there at the time. So after that, I started supporting Barcelona.

First silverware

When I was young, my team won a lot of tournaments but I played for the national team at U16 level and we came third in the Nordic Cup. We played Denmark, Norway, Sweden, Iceland and England were in the tournament as well, although I'm not sure why. It was held in the Faroe Islands.

JAMES FORREST

First goal

I can remember scoring my first goal for Celtic when I was in the under-10s. It was at Barrowfield and it was the first proper game that we played. We were playing 11-a-side but was from 18-yard box to 18-yard box. It was just a really good strike and I have never forgotten it. I was buzzing at the time.

First strip

I can't remember the first one, but I always had about six or seven tops for English and Spanish teams. I had Man United tops and I remember having a Chelsea one. I also had Barca, Real Madrid strips, and even one from Atletico Madrid at one point.

First silverware

At the end of every year, Celtic always used to go on trips abroad and it was good to play against foreign teams. I remember getting to the final one year and we also got to the final of the Villarreal tournament when I was with the U19s. My first winner's medal would have been in the Glasgow Cup in 2008 when I was playing for the U17s. I must have been about 15 or 16 and we beat Rangers 3-1 in Airdrie and I scored.

CHAMPIONSHIP CHEERS

THE THREE-IN-A-ROW CELTS HAD PLENTY TO CELEBRATE WHEN THE CURTAIN CAME DOWN ON A FANTASTIC SEASON.

CELTIC still had seven games left to spare when they sealed a third successive title in sparkling style away to Partick Thistle in late March.

The Hoops played with the authority of champions at Firhill, brushing the Jags aside 5-1 thanks to Anthony Stokes' brace and goals from Liam Henderson, Stefan Johansen and Kris Commons.

It was a fitting way to clinch a 45th league crown after Neil Lennon's men had dominated the Scottish Premiership from day one in the season, with no one else able to match their relentless pace.

The Irishman also made history in becoming only the fourth manager of the club to guide the team to three-in-a-row, following Willie Maley, Jock Stein and Gordon Strachan – exalted company indeed.

And that's an achievement he will always reflect on with great pride, having vacated the Paradise hot-seat in the summer after four years at the helm.

Celtic's consistency was simply remarkable as they stormed to the league summit on the back of some scintillating attacking displays to leave all rivals trailing in their wake.

It took until February 25 for the Bhoys to experience defeat in a narrow 2-1 loss at Aberdeen, when they played almost the entire match with 10 men after Virgil van Dijk's early dismissal.

That denied them the chance to be the first side to go through the entire SPL term unbeaten and become 'Invincibles'. When the campaign ended it was the only blot on the card.

The Hoops did smash some records during the season, though, as Fraser Forster went 1,256 minutes without conceding a goal, surpassing Bobby Clark's 43-year-old Scottish league milestone.

In the process, the English internationalist also eclipsed the great Charlie Shaw's club record of 12 consecutive league shut-outs which had stood for 92 years.

Four Celtic Youth Academy players – Darnell Fisher, Liam Henderson, Eoghan O'Connell and John Herron – were also handed their first full bows

during the season to play their part in the success, with Fisher and Henderson becoming regulars in the first-team squad.

Even after confirming the championship, Celtic were in no mood to canter across the line, notching up several emphatic victories as they built up to Trophy Day in the season finale against Dundee United.

A convincing 3-1 victory over the Terrors saw the Bhoys breach the 100-goal barrier and end the campaign on 99 points. It was the perfect prelude to the presentation of the silverware to captain Scott Brown as the players, backroom staff and supporters celebrated a richly-deserved title triumph in Paradise.

DOT TO DOT

Join up all of the dots in this picture and see if you can identify who this Celt is.
*Indicates new line start (Answer on pages 62/63).

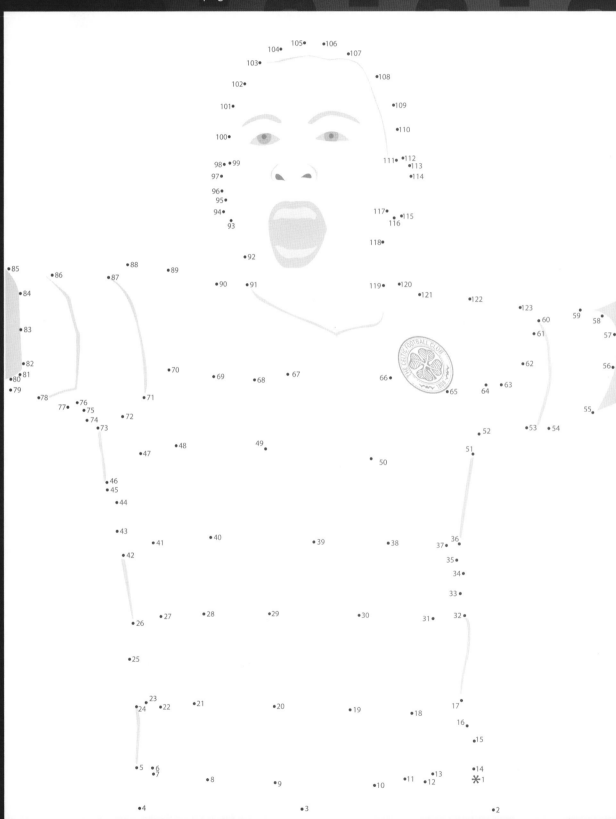

THROUGH THE TRANSFER WINDOW

See if you can match up the Celtic player with the club from which he signed.

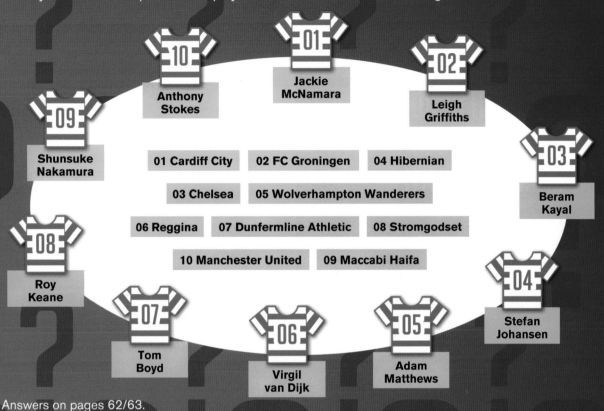

01 Jackie McNamara
02 Leigh Griffiths
03 Beram Kayal
04 Stefan Johansen
05 Adam Matthews
06 Virgil van Dijk
07 Tom Boyd
08 Roy Keane
09 Shunsuke Nakamura
10 Anthony Stokes

01 Cardiff City   02 FC Groningen   04 Hibernian

03 Chelsea   05 Wolverhampton Wanderers

06 Reggina   07 Dunfermline Athletic   08 Stromgodset

10 Manchester United   09 Maccabi Haifa

Answers on pages 62/63.

HENRIK LARSSON
OUT AT THE TOP

EXIT

Henrik left Celtic in the summer of 2004, after seven sensational years at the club. His final game at Paradise was a league clash against Dundee United, where naturally he scored both goals to give Celtic a 2-1 victory. At the end of the game there were tears on the pitch and in the stands on what was a very emotional day. During his last competitive appearance for the Hoops, the Super Swede scored another two goals to help Celtic beat Dunfermline and win the Scottish Cup. There was to be one final bow at Paradise – a farewell game against Sevilla – when the Celtic support said thankyou and goodbye to the Magnificent Seven.

FIVE-IN-A-ROW FOR THE YOUNG HOOPS

CELTIC'S YOUTH ACADEMY POLICY PAYS DIVIDENDS WITH FIFTH SUCCESSIVE TITLE

CELTIC under-20s made it a fantastic five-in-a-row after a dramatic last-day title-clinching victory over Dundee United at Tannadice.

Goals from Jamie Lindsay and Paul McMullan sealed a 2-0 victory over the Terrors, prompting jubilation among the Bhoys.

Described by Development Squad coach Stevie Frail as the most satisfying success of all the championship triumphs, the young Celts showed huge character over the closing weeks of the campaign to retain their crown.

Having suffered a disappointing defeat to Hearts, the youths regrouped to harvest maximum reward from their final three games of the season, including a priceless 2-0 win over Rangers, who only required a share of the spoils to take the title.

SPFL U

CHAM

During the campaign, a full team of Development Squad youngsters departed on loan to garner invaluable competitive experience at clubs in Scotland, England and Ireland, with the likes of Callum McGregor proving a huge hit at Notts County.

This reduced the numbers available for the U20s and left the team with a more youthful composition for their League programme in comparison to their League opponents, many of whom utilised the rule which permitted the use of several over age players.

But there was to be no denying Frail and John Kennedy's young guns, whose resolve, togetherness and will-to-win saw them prevail for a fifth successive season.

And the Bhoys were presented with their prize on the pitch in front of a bumper crowd in Paradise at half-time of the season finale against Dundee United.

Highlights from the campaign included doing the double over Rangers and 5-0 routs of Motherwell and Ross County. But edging a five-goal thriller against St Mirren, when playing practically the entire game with 10 men, proved crucial and will be remembered as one of the standout showings.

But the most pleasing aspect of the season for coaching staff was to see four players rewarded for their excellent performances and make their debut for the first team – Darnell Fisher, Liam Henderson, John Herron and Eoghan O'Connell.

LEAGUE

ONS 2013/14

CELTIC PARK SHINES ON WORLD STAGE

PARADISE PERFECT FOR COMMONWEALTH GAMES OPENING

THE eyes of the world were focused on Celtic Park in July. And Paradise proved to be the perfect venue for the opening ceremony of the Glasgow 2014 Commonwealth Games.

The city hosted the 20th Commonwealth Games, and the sporting extravaganza kicked off with a spectacular opening ceremony at Celtic Park.

Among the highlights of the night were performances by Celtic supporter, Rod Stewart, who sang a special version of *Rhythm of My Heart*, while Susan Boyle sang *Mull of Kintyre*.

Athletes from all the competing countries were greeted warmly into Paradise, with the biggest cheer being reserved for Scotland as the host nation.

And Tonga boxer, Lomalito Moala, won a few Celtic fans when he paraded round the stadium proudly waving the green and white Hoops.

Rod Stewart also performed towards the end of the ceremony, singing his recent hit song, *Can't Stop Me Now*.

And fellow Celtic fan, actor James McAvoy, took to the stage along with Sir Chris Hoy to launch a special appeal for UNICEF's Children of the Commonwealth Fund.

Nicola Benedetti also performed before another famous Celtic fan, Billy Connolly, on the giant screen that stretched across the entire South Stand, paid tribute to late South African president, Nelson Mandela. Billy spoke about Mandela's links to Glasgow going back many years.

There then followed a moving rendition of *Freedom Come All Ye* by South African singer, Pumeza Matshikiza.

Fireworks lighting the East End sky over Paradise signalled to the city, the country and the world that the Glasgow 2014 Commonwealth Games were now open.

LISBON LIONS

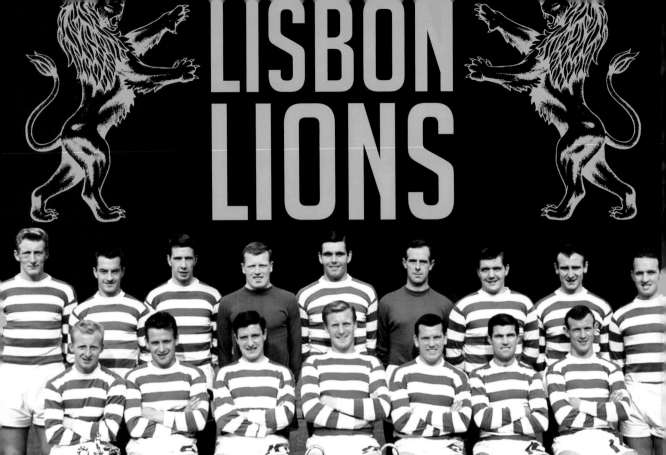

THE Lions returned to Lisbon 47 years on from when they achieved greatness in the Portuguese capital, and once again their visit was a spectacular success.

On May 25, 1967, 11 players all born within 30 miles of Celtic Park defied the odds to sweep aside Inter Milan 2-1 in the Estadio Nacional and became the first British side to become European Champions. It was the greatest day in the history of Celtic Football Club.

The adventurous, swashbuckling style of Jock Stein's side was also considered a victory for football over the defensive, 'Catenaccio' tactics of the Italians. It drew admiration from across the world and sparked a resurgence of attacking football among European football.

The Lions' achievements were never forgotten by the city of Lisbon, and despite the passing of almost half a century, Billy McNeill and his team-mates – sadly minus some of the squad and the backroom staff who are no longer with us – received a warm reception wherever they went on their return in May.

Accompanied by their iconic piece of silverware, the heroes of 1967 were officially welcomed back to the Portuguese capital on Saturday morning at Lisbon City Hall, where they were greeted by representatives of the council and given a guided tour of the building.

They then visited a gallery dedicated to the past European Cup winners along with the official UEFA Champions League museum, happily posing for pictures with locals and supporters of Atletico Madrid and Real Madrid, who were in town ahead of the UEFA Champions League final.

TV crews and journalists were also keen to hear their story and the Bhoys were delighted to tell their tale of triumph to a new audience across the globe.

Special guests in the Estadio da Luz for the showpiece event, the Lions watched Real overcome their city neighbours 4-1 after extra-time in a compelling contest.

But no one will ever roar like the Lions, and the next day they returned to the scene of their stunning success – the mystical Estadio Nacional stadium, which, surreally, is largely preserved in the same state as it was in 1967.

The climax of the trip was a special dinner and reception at the Palacio Hotel in Estoril – their base for their conquest of Europe.

Their presence quickly attracted the attention of a wedding party and the Bhoys were happy to oblige the clamour for pictures from the bride and groom, and guests young and old.

In front of dignitaries from Glasgow, Lisbon and the British Embassy in Portugal, the Lions recalled their memories of making history and spoke of their continued camaraderie, while their anecdotes filled the air with laughter.

The club's charitable tradition and ethos were also highlighted during the event as Celtic FC Foundation handed over 12,000 Euros to benefit three good causes based in the local area.

It was a fitting end to a memorable trip, in which the Lions had proved wonderful ambassadors for Celtic and further enhanced the reputation of the club on foreign shores.

ANSWERS

PAGE 22: SPOT THE DIFFERENCE

PAGE 23: SPFL SEASON 2013/14 QUIZ

1. Anthony Stokes
2. 102
3. St Johnstone
4. Motherwell
5. Dundee United
6. St Johnstone and Dundee United
7. They beat Inverness CT and Partick Thistle 1-0
8. It was 13 games
9. Partick Thistle
10. Kris Commons

PAGE 26: MAZE

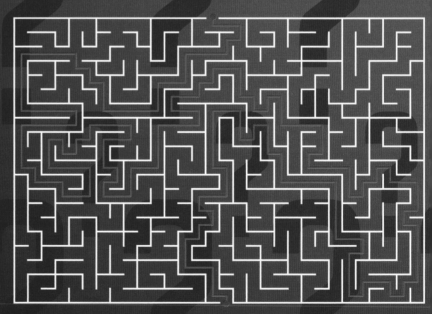